Gravity Won

Kevin M. Clay

Romar Press

Romar Press

3157 CR 518, Stephenville, Texas 76401
publisher@romarpress.com
www.romarpress.com

Cover art: Still from *The Student of Prague*, 1926. Dir. Henrik Galeen. Starring Conrad Veidt,
        Werner Krauss, Elizza La Porta.

Hardover: ISBN 979-8-9921836-2-7
eBook: ISBN 979-8-9921836-3-4

Dedication

For some of my family . . .

Raymond Masten Clay, Sr.
Edna Fenn Clay
Ronald Lee Roberts
LaRita Inez Parks
Raymond Masten Clay, Jr.
David Masten Clay, Sr.
Rachael Havah Clay
Miriam Talya Takver Clay
Elizabeth Baclayo Clay
Robert Mark Clay
Patrick Wayne Clay
Staci Lee Clay

. . . And the coming generations . . .

Acknowledgements

"Shark," "Oresteia," "The Bar Scene," "A Brief Disquisition on the Meaning of Life," "Halloween," "Lazarus," "Properties Of Matter, "[To find the terrible beauty]," "The Dog Won't Have to Sleep on His Potatoes Anymore," retitled here "A Balancing of Accounts," "What About the Beav?" and "Prognostications." *The Langdon Review,* vol. 6, 2009-2010, pp.2-18.

"Jesus Stinks." *Staple.* ed. by Ann Atkinson & Elizabeth Barrett, Autumn 2005, p. 59.

"Before Sleep," "The Rough Economy of Genocide," and "Madonna and Child." *A Literary Bent Magazine.*

"The Mystics of Water and Stone" and "Absolution." *Sulphur River Literary Review.*, ed. by James Michael Robbins, 14.1 (Spring 2003), pp. 40-41.

"Ingenue." *Anthology,* ed. by Chris L. Edwards & Jimmy L. Hood, Jr., vol. 2, Spring 1996, p. 33.

"Gravity Won," "Carswell, 1962," "Lost in the Funhouse," retitled here, "A Testimonial Egg," "Accounts Receivable" and "The Care and Use of the Telephone as an Instrument of Torture." *Anthology,* ed. by Chris L. Edwards & Jimmy L. Hood, Jr., vol. 1, Spring 1995, pp. 61-66.

Foreword

At first I started here about literary matters. You know, stuff as distant from the real *us* as Shin-equi-unninni, the scribe who wrote (or wrote down) the Assyrian recension of *Gilgamesh*, foundational (or moreso) as the *Beowulf* and *Moby Dick*, and other stuff as contemporary and, therefore, exotic as theories of the Modern and the postmodern—but in the end, I thought I'd leave most of that out for now.

The point for me is that the poem is the poem, no more and no less. To understand the poem in any increasingly analytic ways is tantamount to losing it. Baraba Hernnstein-Smith talks in *Contingencies of Value* about her own experience of this in studying Shakespeare's sonnets over the years. The poem is the poem.

TABLE OF CONTENTS

Essay: Life, the Universe, and Everything

"Life, the Universe, and Everything," Douglas Adams says—I do suppose that to be the legitimate scope of art generally. In the end it represents itself alone, whatever constructs we might build upon it: experience of the world embodied in language, and transcripted directly into sharable form, with as much fidelity to truth as possible. I emphatically do not mean truth with a capital "T." This coloring-outside-the-lines, this expanding distance between reader and poem, are the negative consequences of criticism, I think. There are positive ones, too, to be sure—but the point here is other than that.

I have written poetry at least since grade school. How good or bad any of it may have been or may be, at whatever point in time, is not something I feel prepared to answer with any degree of coherence. I could say, in the predictable ways, that *I'm Just Driven to It, or The Muse Moves Me at Odd Times*, but that isn't it—not really. When I was younger, I was aware early that an abstracted gaze into the middle distance would often prompt women (girls really) equally young to be interested in me sexually—but that is just the kind of posturing that I have come to think, to hope, to believe that poetry, or any art worthy of the name "art," ought to eschew. Often enough, I have not eschewed such things: I confess it.

What sort of truth are we trying to get at when we write a poem? Whatever else it may be, it is not critical truth. Not, in my view, Great Moral Truth, either, but quite the obverse. We want—I want—homely and particular truths about ordinary human experience. Don't get me wrong—ordinary experience includes a great many truly atrocious and truly wonderful things. That is, in fact, the whole postmodern thing: how commonplace and utterly banal the outrages of the past have come to be for us, eviscerated as we are with ennui, or if you prefer, nausea: how world-weary we affect to be, and how media-sated we are. We haven't so much seen real tragedy as we've watched it on TV, you know, waiting with ill-concealed impatience for the scheduled football game, Dallas vs. Miami. I feel despair enough that this is so, and more despair at the terrible things we do to one another in large ways and small alike, and at the utter moral and existential cluelessnes of so many people, emphatically including myself, but I do not feel anything like a fatal lassitude. I do not feel ennui: I feel moral outrage, and that's where the political stuff in here comes from because it winds up in the exact opposite of ennui: I want to do something. But, on the other hand, I haven't much more than a clue, myself. So what to do? Well, I can write.

Thus the poem. Meannesses large and small are equally grist for that mill, but still on the scale of individuals. I'm not big on mass movements. Things get quite weird enough even so, when you're looking for the Higgs boson of prosodics and poesy, and also when you aren't. Weirder maybe even than actual physics. No matter: There are wonderful things, too, and about all of that is in the relation of person to nature, or what is much the same thing, person to person.

Sappho knew this, even if Homer (or whomever), did not. These linkages have changed little despite all these intervening centuries; they remain heart and soul of lyric poetry. Wonder and horror commingle in the moist warmness of the meat that moves and speaks, lives and dies, nurtures and murders. Yes, there are sunrises of heartwrenching beauty, the love of a couple, the love of parent and child (my favorite), good food and good company, a fucking rainbow for Christ's own sake—floating dead and bloody up there somewhere above the West—Western Civilization—still yet—and it is all the same. We confuse the rainbow with that bleeding Catholic Christ for good and sufficient reason. The same with terror and bliss. The Maenaeds pursuing the hapless sacrifice, the crowds shrieking for the blood of witches are not materially different from brownshirted Nazis, or I dare say from the crowds that gather in Huntsville, outside the maximum-security Walls unit on execution dates, here in my own, my beloved, my detested, my outraged Texas, but the same creatures, devil and angel, accomplish every bit of it with no need for magics of any sort. Yet there *are* dreams and visions. So many people celebrate so exuberantly the new death, but they celebrate their own beating hearts, too, only they don't know it. Robert Graves' White Goddess is into that moil—and all the Gael intensity of Joyce, of Beckett, of

Dylan Thomas through my own oh-so-American Scotch-Irishness. And yet stupidity, O my children, remains both potent and abundant.

I love my country and my heritage. But I do *not* love them like a fool.

I remember my own dismay when people seemed so happy that thousands had been killed on this day or that in Afghanistan or Iraq, or Vietnam. "Snow and corruption know them," Borges wrote of the Falkland War--but never a word from the uniformed high and mighty about the question this most obviously provokes: embraced in the corrupt anonymity of death, are they still enemies? I do not speak of the Brits so much regarding the Falklands as of my own country and its own interminable wars, though I see little difference. I wish I could say I opposed all of these messes from the start, but I didn't --I hoped at the tine they --the governments, you know--were telling the truth, I hoped we could give Hershey bars to kids and make the world safe for democracy. But no. They were lying again, just as they had about Vietnam. National origins and race are not, to me, significant distinctions: I really mean it when I say we are all human, though this has often in recent times been treated as if it were some sort of tree-hugging joke, something from Cheech and Chong. The fact is that these killings are carried out in our names, you know, and on our behalf, whatever your "our" may be—mine is American—but in the end they will only, as Donne very well knew (though clearly we do not) diminish us all, all the more. That hasn't changed, but this other thing—poetry, the attempt to know it all well enough to deal with it all more-or-less constructively—has not changed, either. Not in the important ways. We still need and want to *explain*.

The terrain we inhabit is on the far side of Hitler, and the far side, too, of Hiroshima and Auschwitz, where things have fallen apart indeed, and grow sillier—or more absurd, if you prefer that—with each day that passes. In this cringing new world of ours, we don't really need Hitler, AKA Modernism gone stark rabid insane, nor the Satan he has so effectively replaced—we're all crazy (there's that "all" thing again) right from Jump Street. Aren't we? I say we are, and it is that condition, madness, which leads to so much self-reference exactly because there is so very little in the way of shared belief and opinion, leading in turn to fragmentation and division, and that is the postmodern condition entire—but it hasn't been in flower long enough to get a capital letter, or killed nearly enough people, but by and by, who knows? With a few more Rwandas, Iraqs, and Yugoslavias, and I daresay, Ukraines, we will get there.

Gravity Won

Kevin M. Clay

Romar Press

Romar Press

3157 CR 518, Stephenville, Texas 76401
publisher@romarpress.com
www.romarpress.com

Cover art: Still from *The Student of Prague*, 1926. Dir. Henrik Galeen. Starring Conrad Veidt,
Werner Krauss, Elizza La Porta.

Hardover: ISBN
eBook:

Dedication

For some of my family . . .

Raymond Masten Clay, Sr.
Edna Fenn Clay
Ronald Lee Roberts
LaRita Inez Parks
Raymond Masten Clay, Jr.
David Masten Clay, Sr.
Rachael Havah Clay
Miriam Talya Takver Clay
Elizabeth Baclayo Clay
Robert Mark Clay
Patrick Wayne Clay
Staci Lee Clay

. . . And the coming generations . . .

Acknowledgements

"Shark," "Oresteia," "The Bar Scene," "A Brief Disquisition on the Meaning of Life," "Halloween," "Lazarus," "Properties Of Matter, "[To find the terrible beauty]," "The Dog Won't Have to Sleep on His Potatoes Anymore," retitled here "A Balancing of Accounts," "What About the Beav?" and "Prognostications." *The Langdon Review*, vol. 6, 2009-2010, pp.2-18.

"Jesus Stinks." *Staple*. ed. by Ann Atkinson & Elizabeth Barrett, Autumn 2005, p. 59.

"Before Sleep," "The Rough Economy of Genocide," and "Madonna and Child" *A Literary Bent Magazine*.

"The Mystics of Water and Stone" and "Absolution." *Sulphur River Literary Review*., ed. by James Michael Robbins, 14.1 (Spring 2003), pp. 40-41.

"Ingenue." *Anthology*, ed. by Chris L. Edwards & Jimmy L. Hood, Jr., vol. 2, Spring 1996, p. 33.

"Gravity Won," "Carswell, 1962," "Lost in the Funhouse," retitled here, "A Testimonial Egg," "Accounts Receivable" and "The Care and Use of the Telephone as an Instrument of Torture.o" *Anthology*, ed. by Chris L. Edwards & Jimmy L. Hood, Jr., vol. 1, Spring 1995, pp. 61-66.

Foreword

At first I started here about literary matters. You know, stuff as distant from the real *us* as Shin-equi-unninni, the scribe who wrote (or wrote down) the Assyrian recension of *Gilgamesh*, foundational (or moreso) as the *Beowulf* and *Moby Dick*, and other stuff as contemporary and, therefore, exotic as theories of the Modern and the postmodern—but in the end, I thought I'd leave most of that out for now.

The point for me is that the poem is the poem, no more and no less. To understand the poem in any increasingly analytic ways is tantamount to losing it. Baraba Hernnstein-Smith talks in *Contingencies of Value* about her own experience of this in studying Shakespeare's sonnets over the years. The poem is the poem.

TABLE OF CONTENTS

Essay: Life, the Universe, and Everything

"Life, the Universe, and Everything," Douglas Adams says—I do suppose that to be the legitimate scope of art generally. In the end it represents itself alone, whatever constructs we might build upon it: experience of the world embodied in language, and transcripted directly into sharable form, with as much fidelity to truth as possible. I emphatically do not mean truth with a capital "T." This coloring-outside-the-lines, this expanding distance between reader and poem, are the negative consequences of criticism, I think. There are positive ones, too, to be sure—but the point here is other than that.

I have written poetry at least since grade school. How good or bad any of it may have been or may be, at whatever point in time, is not something I feel prepared to answer with any degree of coherence. I could say, in the predictable ways, that *I'm Just Driven to It, or The Muse Moves Me at Odd Times*, but that isn't it—not really. When I was younger, I was aware early that an abstracted gaze into the middle distance would often prompt women (girls really) equally young to be interested in me sexually—but that is just the kind of posturing that I have come to think, to hope, to believe that poetry, or any art worthy of the name "art," ought to eschew. Often enough, I have not eschewed such things: I confess it.

What sort of truth are we trying to get at when we write a poem? Whatever else it may be, it is not critical truth. Not, in my view, Great Moral Truth, either, but quite the obverse. We want—I want—homely and particular truths about ordinary human experience. Don't get me wrong—ordinary experience includes a great many truly atrocious and truly wonderful things. That is, in fact, the whole postmodern thing: how commonplace and utterly banal the outrages of the past have come to be for us, eviscerated as we are with ennui, or if you prefer, nausea: how world-weary we affect to be, and how media-sated we are. We haven't so much seen real tragedy as we've watched it on TV, you know, waiting with ill-concealed impatience for the scheduled football game, Dallas vs. Miami. I feel despair enough that this is so, and more despair at the terrible things we do to one another in large ways and small alike, and at the utter moral and existential cluelessnes of so many people, emphatically including myself, but I do not feel anything like a fatal lassitude. I do not feel ennui: I feel moral outrage, and that's where the political stuff in here comes from because it winds up in the exact opposite of ennui: I want to do something. But, on the other hand, I haven't much more than a clue, myself. So what to do? Well, I can write.

Thus the poem. Meannesses large and small are equally grist for that mill, but still on the scale of individuals. I'm not big on mass movements. Things get quite weird enough even so, when you're looking for the Higgs boson of prosodics and poesy, and also when you aren't. Weirder maybe even than actual physics. No matter: There are wonderful things, too, and about all of that is in the relation of person to nature, or what is much the same thing, person to person.

Sappho knew this, even if Homer (or whomever), did not. These linkages have changed little despite all these intervening centuries; they remain heart and soul of lyric poetry. Wonder and horror commingle in the moist warmness of the meat that moves and speaks, lives and dies, nurtures and murders. Yes, there are sunrises of heartwrenching beauty, the love of a couple, the love of parent and child (my favorite), good food and good company, a fucking rainbow for Christ's own sake—floating dead and bloody up there somewhere above the West—Western Civilization—still yet—and it is all the same. We confuse the rainbow with that bleeding Catholic Christ for good and sufficient reason. The same with terror and bliss. The Maenaeds pursuing the hapless sacrifice, the crowds shrieking for the blood of witches are not materially different from brownshirted Nazis, or I dare say from the crowds that gather in Huntsville, outside the maximum-security Walls unit on execution dates, here in my own, my beloved, my detested, my outraged Texas, but the same creatures, devil and angel, accomplish every bit of it with no need for magics of any sort. Yet there *are* dreams and visions. So many people celebrate so exuberantly the new death, but they celebrate their own beating hearts, too, only they don't know it. Robert Graves' White Goddess is into that moil—and all the Gael intensity of Joyce, of Beckett, of

Dylan Thomas through my own oh-so-American Scotch-Irishness. And yet stupidity, O my children, remains both potent and abundant.

I love my country and my heritage. But I do *not* love them like a fool.

I remember my own dismay when people seemed so happy that thousands had been killed on this day or that in Afghanistan or Iraq, or Vietnam. "Snow and corruption know them," Borges wrote of the Falkland War--but never a word from the uniformed high and mighty about the question this most obviously provokes: embraced in the corrupt anonymity of death, are they still enemies? I do not speak of the Brits so much regarding the Falklands as of my own country and its own intermnninable wars, though I see little difference. I wish I could say I opposed all of these messes from the start, but I didn't --I hoped at the tine they --the governments, you know--were telling the truth, I hoped we could give Hershey bars to kids and make the world safe for democracy. But no. They were lying again, just as they had about Vietnam. National origins and race are not, to me, significant distinctions: I really mean it when I say we are all human, though this has often in recent times been treated as if it were some sort of tree-hugging joke, something from Cheech and Chong. The fact is that these killings are carried out in our names, you know, and on our behalf, whatever your "our" may be—mine is American—but in the end they will only, as Donne very well knew (though clearly we do not) diminish us all, all the more. That hasn't changed, but this other thing—poetry, the attempt to know it all well enough to deal with it all more-or-less constructively—has not changed, either. Not in the important ways. We still need and want to *explain.*

The terrain we inhabit is on the far side of Hitler, and the far side, too, of Hiroshima and Auschwitz, where things have fallen apart indeed, and grow sillier—or more absurd, if you prefer that—with each day that passes. In this cringing new world of ours, we don't really need Hitler, AKA Modernism gone stark rabid insane, nor the Satan he has so effectively replaced—we're all crazy (there's that "all" thing again) right from Jump Street. Aren't we? I say we are, and it is that condition, madness, which leads to so much self-reference exactly because there is so very little in the way of shared belief and opinion, leading in turn to fragmentation and division, and that is the postmodern condition entire—but it hasn't been in flower long enough to get a capital letter, or killed nearly enough people, but by and by, who knows? With a few more Rwandas, Iraqs, and Yugoslavias, and I daresay, Ukraines, we will get there.

Gravity Won

And Larry had wings this night,
That sent him leaping over the road's embankment,
And soaring like the eagle he never was,
Over, and across, and higher still,
Until it seemed that gravity's embrace
Would sullenly surrender.
And his clunker, battered as it was,
Would lift on crackling pillars of fire.

And Larry would smile inanely
With cracked brown teeth—
His green eyes wide, his boy's face stunned—
Away from anger, bondage, sorrow, grief.
But of course, when it was over, gravity won.

1989

Accounts Receivable

Contracts of affection
might be compacts of depravity. One
is not unlike the other.
The house you rule. The horse you ride.
The whore of your convenience.

      Moonlit clouds beyond
      my bedroom window, obese
      with possibility. God damn you.

It all comes off. Piece by
piece. Articles of clothing. Articles
in *Ladies' Home Journal.* Imperfect accounting,
accounts received. Closed out.
A dead number. The ATM won't take my card.
I'm sucked dry.

      Nude figures in a still garden.
      The same moon. Some flowers
      do open in the night. Music.
      A waltz between kisses. God damn you.

Increments of affection, struck off
in decrements of abuse. A buyout,
leveraged of that mutual fund, that
pays in diminishing percent. It all
comes off. Not so special a delivery,
moistened with your limber tongue.

      Remembrances of breast and thighs
      and slick, sweet entries, in that column.
      And an axe slices cleanly the stem
      of a rose. Imperfect erasures
      gloss the theft. We are a palimpsest, geologic.
      God damn you.

Bubbles do burst. Discounting resistance,
objects of unlike weight do fall

at identical velocity. Economics
is not an exact science.

     God damn your perfume.
     God damn my readiness for more.

1991

The Use and Care of the Telephone as an Instrument of Torture

Yesterday I saw Jesus, in a
phone booth. He said he was calling this friend
of his, to tell her. That he loved her.
Missed her. Needed her.
Horribly. Like nails pulled
from yielding flesh. Like a slug of soured wine.
Like some triumphant laurel gone
sudden thorns and twigs. His ache
for her. To touch her. See her. Hear her
say the words to him, and say them back to her again.
Was like the keen edge, the razor tip
of a spear, sliding liquid,
almost sexual,
between the third and fourth rib
into the left lung. A wound
that bleeds, and wheezes
almost words. He said,
she isn't home,
a balloon of sad words.
He left a message,
heart sick, blood simple,
on her answering machine. And then,
hanging up, he said,
oh hell. Romance.

1993

A Testimonial Egg

Well, here we are. Karl and I.
Worried like fat old hens
with the new-born minute
chirping away the time.
Chirping, chirping. Brief testaments—
and purple—out of reordered time's
last syllable.
Karl laid an egg he can't fight.
I can't fight.

An insensate passage
of moment to moment
just will not be
reversed. And time's
continual regicide leads us on.
Like a lady leads a dog,
from one quivering crouch
to the next. It is
a form of foul subtraction
that trims root and branch
to necessity. And we chirp on,
get of the same eggs,
trapped forever
by a bloody-minded clock.

1993

Ingenue

It was one hell of a play, you know.
Hero and heroine
cast to fit a look, a glance, a crabwise
creep after sense and meaning. Poor fools.

Knew not the gist that waited
in the wings; a crab indeed.
Cruel claws, segmented stalks
waving in the ether: shrill signals sent, that
burrow indeed. My carcinomic angel,
riot of cells, wilding gaggle, that
drools pavementwise, not replete.
I'll have your guts for brunch, if you please.
On toast, with marmalade.

Oh, she drowned. Her garments,
fit, to be sure, for an ingénue,
winglike, floated in the water, and
bore her awhile up. But down now,
down they go, and she down with them,
angel in the mud. No curtain call
for you, dear one. While on the catwalks above,
sneering Hamlet smirks in silence, sniggering.
Win one for the Gipper.

1993

Carswell, 1962

We lived in a flight path.
Vast birds flew over us,
freighted with lethal eggs.
It was the warm autumn
of a cold war.

In school, we were herded
To the halls.
Small sheep, ripe
for shearing. We lay our
books open
over our heads, that were
tucked in
between our bended knees

Would the knowledge
spill into our heads
fast enough
that way?

1994

Absolute Zero

It's an empty place,
and so cold.
The wind bites shrewdly.
Nothing in the gaps.
What there is, isn't enough.
Where do I go?
Where will I shelter?
What is the storm that
Flails and tears?
The terrible thing she has done.

1994

Anguish

Weather curdling in the sky blue-black
A frozen riot. Fallen all, with such
a disgraceful crash. Scurry like fleas in fur.
A ferris wheel we tumble off
of at the top, no impact.
A perpendicular merry-go-round
that launches
at escape velocity,
no lift-off,
mere falling.
Always rolling down,
no impact. Games you might win,
but can't,
prizes you might take,
but won't, and
everywhere, the sure-footed tumble
of the gymnast
shod with lead.
Gravity wins.

1994

Oresteia

We've tumbled mighty Corinth down, into tears and blood, while
    justice,
that bitch dog, anyone's Friday night piece, sockets oozing pus,
breeds flies. She drapes her eyes with a filthy rag, clutches,
impotent, her scale. One nod only to propriety, and common
    fucking sense.

You do remember?

Furies all, they waited. He would have patiently to bear
whatever stripes those grinning hags elected to bestow,
all to spite the dying that was all the loving Clytemnestra
and Agamemnon could ever do. If hearts smoldered ardently
on *that* altar, burnt offerings to greedy gods, they did not smolder

for either one of those.

There are rituals much bitterer. Commonplace as resentment.
Parents, children, kings, presidents, princes, and premiers,
not only permit, but insist. Crescendos in the flesh, reduced to
    passages
of great beasts through narrow places. The scorpion folded in the
    sheet
savors of what it stings; only that done unto and doers all are in
    fact

the same sweet flesh.

A sin, a crime, and *your* choice. Not whether or not to be tainted
    so
with Cain's bequest, or Christ's prohibition, but to choose
which stain you'd rather bear. No law or statute stays
the hand poised to stab. He *had* killed her, but if he had not,
there would still have been enough to warrant blood.

No light to see by. Refractories of gray

break into primaries of white; the rituals of murder in the mass

have changed *us*, since we are no more worthy of the classics.
So Bloom would have it. But fate is only
an old woman, enrobed in black patience,
who does not care, but casts the chances

like shards slicing into bloodless ice,
and always someone else who pays.

1994

The Rough Economy of Genocide

Tutsi to Hutu, Hutu to Tutsi, they came peddling hatred like a
      bicycle.
Wives with axes, murderous drudges, husbands bearing bats.
And closed up the doors of the schoolhouse to set the place afire.
How that must have looked! The screams of the children, unseen
in the horror of the flames. And perhaps thin, winged shapes
of children's books like butterflies ablaze, flying
through the air with the smoke, flapping.

What are needed most are companionable swine, and a trough
to root in. I mostly fear my own ignorance, far more than any
      mob.
That is the flabbiest of devils. Yet not so feared as the easy death
that knows nothing, had on the sleight, somehow and strangely at
the same hand.

Do screams of outrage, fear, horror stream all that
      way?
Like clouds, from the far-off of the world, tearing like a high wind
past the billboards, the invisible murmurs of microwaves, the
      whisper
of cell phones, the delicate finesse of the GPS satellite, ripping a
      hole into
matter and time. Each decrement of abuse betrayed to further
      excess
by the one before, when the first were the simpleminded whacks of
a blade, but the last could eat the planet whole.

Mercy frailer still than breath. Let me not miss anything on TV.
It has gone so far, gone on so long, that cruelty has become
banal merely, and I grow bored with atrocities so silly, so absurd in
      their scope,
they force out not outrage, but a giggle of disbelief.
Because I know despite myself: that bubbles do burst.

Discounting resistance, objects of like weight do fall
at identical velocity. And like economics, murder is far
from an exact science.

1994

Jesus Stinks

It was a short trip. Jesus sat in the bow. He tapped the phylactery strapped on His arm and smiled. He shook His forelocks at me and leered. He scratched idly with long, untrimmed fingernails at the scabs around the nails driven into His wrists. He hiked back the sleeves of His long, black, fur-trimmed coat, and He tapped with one finger at the second phylactery strapped around His forehead. He smiled at me stupidly. Coy brambles peeked in the gap between the strap and His enormous fur hat. The hat was a snug fit—it pushed a thorn here and there into His flesh, and He bled black blood down His face. He leaked in a thousand places, all over the boat.

And He scratched at His filthy feet, too. One had a crusted, oozing hole through the ankle, and a long bloody nail stuck out of both sides of the other. His toenails needed clipping and He had a fungus in them and His feet stank. He stank, like an open grave. The fur trim on the hem of His coat was scruffy—hide showing through in patches, poorly cured: it stank almost as badly as the rest, as—well, *Him*. And He kept on saying over and over, Only for you, babe. All for you, only for you.

Yeah, sure, I said. And He hiked up His coat and scratched savagely at His crotch through the loincloth. I guess He had company in there, huh? Needed dipping, like a dog or sheep. It was all just too—too. *Physical*, you know? Maybe we could do something about Him, yes? Because really, it *has* been a long trip, after all.

1995

Sunday Dinner

Old Joe Death ate chicken with us Sundays. He sat in my father's
chair, and passing to the left, said: take, eat. Obdurate flesh like it
   is,
I'd ask him a question or two while I ate mine, could I only

muster the resolve that night. Not that he ever deigned to answer,
   really,
with anything you could use. Yet what are we, any of us, if not
   witnesses?
Joe himself, a mover and a shaker, asks if it is as noble as we
   suppose to tilt

at windmills. Might as well slam your head into unyielding stone,
   he says.
Damage to the brain stem can result, which causes one to assume
an idiot grin we can hardly call out-of-place. I said to him, Joe, you
   mean

like *yours*, Joe? Why worry over a guest, I thought, who is, after
   all, a
mere abstraction. No idle or random insult, surely, but purposeful
   entire. At this
—shreds and curls of flesh falling like rain—Joe's grin got a bit
   more ghastly,

a tooth fell out, his scalp split, his bony face dissolved. A mass of
   wormy meal,
and frogs, croaking musically, arrived to squat hungrily, and
   serenade his
dissolution with croaks. Well. Joe waved a half-chewed drumstick
   while a snake

crawled in one eye and out his fast-dissolving ear. You know, he
   said, there's more
between you and this chicken than anyone but the chicken knows.
   And Dad
said to him nervously, would you like some yams? Joe always
   loved the yams.

1999

The Rubble at Delphi

The brush rolls out like carpet, going on for miles.
Crushed space and squatted heat, a total immersion in
shrieked prayers, all these hysteric shouts while all drown,
all, in the sacred poverty of spirit. Holy ignorance
baptized long since, by the splatter of tongues inchoate
with desire, where mesquite on the banks, aromatic,
claws at a shredded sky. It was redolent
of sandalwood in a dry place. A bargain indeed.
A contract with depravity, made, you know,

only to be broken with lies. A rubble of broken idols,
flakes of paint and dust of stones tickle the nose,
while slick teeth white as bone, streaked red in firelight,
clack at the credulous; no probing tongue so
apt to tease out secrets like these, the smiling,
extrovert proselytes of a new crusade.
All parts of the body marshaled to the singular event,
in earnest of an older, wiser intent.

Would you dance with the Maenaeds at camp meeting?
Right *there*, where all supplicants, we plead,
wheedling out in the day's tongue, the day's importuning.
And smiling, oh always smiling,
wash with a grinning slurp that
ever-hungry mouth. The common coin of the purchase
is the need, and importunate rows
all singing *ave maria*, for the puzzlements of flesh, *te deum*.
The crust of bread neither staff nor stuff, the broad leaf
held up against the rain, not equal to it. When
two feet are no more enough to hold up anyone,
the cracked clay merely, at the broken end of the stone.

2000

The Course of True Love

I ate it all, every morsel,
swallowed it down smooth as grease,
coating the stomach,
my own libidinous bismuth,
hot pink, hot blood.
I did it so I could somehow
keep it all down.

But the slick chalk-sweetness
Won me out at last,
and up it came, in a great steaming geyser.
It splattered the floor,
dripped in curds off the table, dripped
in tacky streamers
down my chin. And

I sat there on the chair, a lump
awaiting lumpectomy,
stinking in the pink ooze, and then,
from the sandy berms without,
a *kampfgruppen* of politic ants,
marching in goose-step,
trooped in, and licked up
every precious drop
to haul off for storage,
a hedge against inflation.

2000

Crucifixion, 7:00 pm

Nail him up. Let him whimper a few hours, stapled
to all those tomorrows, all those pogroms to be,
and let him hang, at least until the curtain tears.

How many passions did you play today?
Standing outside the neatly paved courtyard,
where they held the trial, how many times did you deny him?
Faith abandoned like a room, to spiderwebs and dust.
How would we ever know it, if the martyr did
promise his all to Satan, just as the axe fell?
We mustn't speak of such things, you know, for this
is a solemn occasion.

The nails let flow
the wiser, older blood, and none of it was ours,
all of it was his. A mind like a throat,
all swallow. How the hell should I have known?

Crafty, the majordomo slams hard
the door just as sentence is pronounced.
Everyone looks, and crafty still, he hides the key
right *there*, where no one would ever think to find it.

2000

Face

Our hungers
run in packs, like dogs or wolves,
bringing down a wounded thing,
pinwheels of blood and thrashing limbs,
a crash in the snow and all red.
See the gorgeous, spouting blood.

Time will pass. The sun rises and sets across the sky
predictably in its prescribed arc.
Clouds march, wherever it is
clouds go; the hands of clocks, move.

Still yet the concupiscence lurks
in the space behind my eyes.
Such hunger is a tyrant, devourer of
fool and wise alike. An endless, careening
fall
into
the
past.
Love me.
Fuck me.
Love's dog, howling.
Scratching at fleas.

2001

Lazarus

When Jesus beckoned him, Lazarus rose from the dead,
just as he was ordered. And obediently, stood in the door awhile,
fingering nervously the rock just rolled aside, looking round sort

of baffled, wondering, what *is* that terrible smell? The mess
on the stone bier must have made him all the more curious
because of the sheet he was wrapped in, damp and stinking,
while Jesus, never the patient one, waited tapping one foot,
thinking: My public awaits

They never tell you this part.

                              Eventually, Lazarus puzzled
it out, and as it came slowly clear just what had been
done to him, he turned to his Benefactor, who waited all smiles,
hand extended to slap the back: hee-HEE! Fellow well met. And
Lazarus, softly, as one recently awakened, murmured only:
You show-off. You silly, showboating ass.

2002

Some Old Movie

Comes out of some old movie, the whisper of
my mother's name in tones I'd rather not have heard.
And all I can say, from some old movie again,
in a reedy whisper, is this:
I am the fool for Christ.
I am the Paraclete of Caborca.
I am the wild-haired boy.

Not like that exactly, but close. Patches out of books,
a vagrant snatch of an old song, a game no one plays
any more. Something my mother once said. Angrily.
And my father shouting in a weepy voice, words like clubs,
that drub the heart's tattoo, and the blood comes,
and oh,
then breaks the day
into shards of sunlight
pouring through the window,
like ice arrested in its motion.

2002

Madonna and Child

The young mother cared so much about her son she kept him in the closet on a shelf. She was only trying to keep him safe. She knew the world was full of devils, and she had the tracks to prove it, and the well-bruised genitals so cruelly used. Can't be too careful with those devils. Of course, the devils had looked just like the boys she went out to the party with, the ones who gave her good drugs, but that was just a devil's trick. You can tell them by their red eyes. So she put the baby on the shelf and left him there, where he would be safe. She thought the State might come, as they had come for her, and take the baby to a series of foster homes, such as she had grown up in. That was OK too, so long as the men didn't mess with you. The men in several of those homes were always messing with her, and she learned to just wait it out until they sent her on to the next. No one believed, when she said. The man's wife least of all. Maybe the man there, the next man, wouldn't mess with you. There were devils in all the mirrors, too. And the ponds in the park where she asked people for money. And in puddles of water in the streets. They waited, just far enough away to not be seen.

So after the baby was safe, she went out the door to the street where the boys waited, and they had some more drugs. They were just boys then, not overly bright but not habitually cruel, and didn't turn into monsters until she came to regret having gone with them. She came to regret having gone with them when she came to herself with one of them on top of her, grunting and pushing, as she herself came to regret ever having been at all at all such times, and it was at just such a time was when the devils came the worst, or they all became devils. The drugs were so good because when she used them she forgot things and plenty of things needed forgetting, and always there was more and more and more to forget. She prayed to God all the time, but somehow God never answered, but always there were drugs, always there was forgetting, and forgetting was very important. The boys were willing to give her drugs always, and always she came to regret taking them, but always there was the forgetting that came with the drugs, and the one thing she could remember was the terrible, aching need to forget. Thank God for drugs.

And she kept right on at it. She had an apartment, or really a room, with a closet, and the man came by and he collected his rent in the same way she got the boys to give her the drugs, only he was old and he took longer. While he took longer, she stared at the ceiling and counted. She counted up into the thousands, a number each time the old man grunted, each time her head bounced its little bounce on the dirty pillow, and that way it went a little faster until finally he was through and he left her, loins rich with wet, and that way there wasn't quite as *much* to forget, because it all went into the counting and then all she remembered was the counting. Measuring off the day into time. It was a form of technology. Some day she would learn computers. Some day she would be a beautician. She decided the man was a devil, too. There was a lot of money in computers. She had been young and pretty, but very quickly that faded. Each day was about like the one before it. Something in the closet had begun to smell.

2003

Properties of Matter

I can feel all the heat at
the world's core;
It is this the plumb-bob
points to
so resolutely.

I think of my
fingertips sliding down your spine,
you shiver. The earth quakes.
One mouth opens to the other,
eyes close on
flesh rising like spring.
Gorgeous with color,
a flower
to be picked in the Spring.
I would quaff you
as a bee or butterfly,
in the fullness of things.
As from a cup,
and never see the bottom.

2003

What about the Beav?

We heard in March that Wally had been killed at Húe,
on the banks of the Perfume River, the day before he
turned nineteen. No birthday cake needed. His piece, broken,
lies on scorched ground.
Ward and June were quiet the balance of the season,
and the Beav pretty much on his own.

Broken by the wheel they rode. It was the year,
smiling everywhere but his eyes,
Eddie Haskell obtained the local concession
for Columbian coke.
His mules brought it in by the ton,
and had so much fun in process, by and by they
felt not a thing at all, which made the business easier
to transact, surely. While the Beaver, furtive in the park,
smoked ordinary reefer behind a tree. Caught, then,
in the act—foul corruptor of our glorious Republic—
he jumped the fence at a bound, trying to escape the
smiling yokel bearing down on him. Who bore handcuffs
and sage advice. The way it is, you know.
That boy never could get away with anything.

And so there it was: that some things change
not at all, while others. Oh, God. So fast. Each night
of all nights before, Ward and June hove heavy sighs
screenward the TV.
All that shaking of wise heads, heavier still, availed nothing.
The times were still the times. Good night, Chet, said David.
And good night David, said Chet. Others slept,
that fabled year, oh, very soundly.

But the desperation to *feel*—something, anything,
did give his dayglo dreams a certain urgency—a longing
for *truth*, with that capital "T,"
bright to bursting, and rainbows gushed like water
out of his eyes, the glyphs of
some new language learnt by osmosis
via headphone, a rebel praxis informed with words

sprung fully armed into life, with only
a little brain powder. A touch of narcotic. Clever enough,
yes, but even *those* poets, ramped to the gills,
could not bespeak entire
the fullness of the hollowness within.

Yawning cavities of red meat, redolent of deaths inexplicably
grand, but also empty. The seat of the soul
he struggled on with, searching out somehow, but so, so
blindly, to fill it, to fulfill it, all unlettered and unwise,
staring without, within,
that blinkless, tearless eye, declaiming: what cannot be seen, shall
    be heard,
shall sing: good night, Jimi, good night, Janis, good night, Jim.
Careful now. Tell too much truth, they will shoot you.
Look at Jesus. Look at the good Reverend. Look at
little Bobby and Big John.

Followed by a moment of silence.

And the Beav?

June has asked that every birthday since, while Ward smiles
only a little, just enough to humor her, but not so much she knows
his bitterest thought: that 1963 should never have ended at all,
least of all with gunshots in the wide plaza, because
we believed *everything* then. We swallowed it all down whole.

But so: I ask you, what else could have been done?
When things that seemed that good
had gone that horribly, horribly wrong?
And all with good intentions—*WINK, WINK*—
—yet have we not trod, again and again,
the road that's paved with those?
One night to a tune less beloved, the Beav danced the overdose
dance, *STEP*—one-two—*STEP*—one-two, and if that made
the winter in his soul less real, the truths of suffering and pain,
Live Via Satellite or not, in vivid NBC color or not,
more real, so do
they enter still yet

the black-and-white worlds of our most depraved indulgences,
that overween much more than mere pride.
And so much more the pity
that so it has been, and so will it be again.

Beaver,
what are you talking about?

Happy birthday, Wally.
Good night, Chet.

2003

Shark

Memories may come like dreams, but they feed
like sharks, mouths snapping amid the schools
of flashing tuna. Death waiting with razor teeth, between
each rapid heartbeat. I have seen her, standing on
the deck dry shod. She carries a book in one hand, but does
not read it. She said she'd never seen a vision. I tried to
tell her how. There is only the leap to make, over
the side and down. It used to make me afraid, to think she might
do that: all history there for the seeing, if only you have the eyes.

The shoals are thick with scum off Aransas, and hate
is so exhausting. It makes us a burnt offering, chaos
of thinking. How the monster hated its maker!
Your knife was sharp, but also lingering and slow. Was I *like* this?
Before the dissection? Did I hate before *anyone*, so implacably?
Death is neither cloud nor cave, but an ocean. Sharks prowl it.
Other things with equal teeth.
Sleep eludes me still.

New Orleans is over there, basting like a crab in the sun.
If your eyes could see what mine have, it is *you* would fear.
But let sleep come. Blow out your lamps. My mother waits, and
the gulf is such a muddy water. Less deep than altogether
enclosed. What comes ashore is the discarded, the thrown
away. A nautical sort of vivisection, an epic
exploration, Vesalius rather than Aphrodite, risen
half-shelled from the waves.
How long does anything last, really?

2004

The Hanging Moon

Gnawing by rote at the wire, the glowering bitch,
passing fond, teats fat
with milk, no thought but of the squirming whelps
she harbors in her belly. Throws itself like fury at the walls.

She haunts these rooms like a childhood pet,
fondly remembered, missed, dead.
Old dogs good to no one,
themselves least of all. Better,
better by far, to put them out of the way.

The days turn like a planet
falling around the sun: years pass. It's a fool
that places such faith in anyone—yet it is the nature
of a dog, to lick the hand that strikes it. Just so,
to hear them laughing in the night,
at the dead-dog dragging of the days.

A dog is love's fool, wagging
its stump where before, there may have been
the perfect tail. Small grinning children with
rubber bands and knives. Scissors.

Then somehow, it manages to *smile*.
You wouldn't think a dog could do that.
But it can. Scratching at
phantom fleas, biting through hair at its own flesh,
making a feast. And howling, oh, God, the
howling. For no apparent reason the neighbors can
see, at the bloated, hanging moon.

2004

Before Sleep

A claw in the throat, that digs where
all the words piled up, unspoken.

2004

Halloween

October was crueler than I knew,
a month of burnt earth and dead trees,
counting up the day's catch
of picked bones, and all about like incense,
the sad, strange sweetness of betrayal.
Skeletons of crepe and tack dangled from porches.
In a star of yielding wax, a plastic head with
glowing eyes, red streaks down the faux,
parchment-colored bone, sat motionless
on a dinner plate. From its still mouth,
rich mocking laughter.

It was very like swallowing a stone. Like
embracing 40 knives or more bundled edge-out.
You can't deny mere flesh, merely because
it is flesh, because: flesh will tell.

Jack-o-lanterns grinned at the windows,
leering with gapped teeth. Down on the tracks,
a group of children stumbled clumsily
in their costumes. They moved
when the train came. They clambered down,
athwart the piled aggregate roadbed, while
humming and hooting, the diesel roared past.
The children stood like stones to watch it go,
got up in haughty silliness. A boy in white
carried a toy saber. The train gone, he laid about him
like a champion, while the rails yet squealed from
the weight. The sword hummed fiercely,
noises from a movie. It glowed lengthwise
in the dark autumn air.

2004

Cleaning Up the Mess

Some things we all need, but she wanted a
stone promise, some absolute commitment from
the gods, that nothing would ever, ever go awry
with her mooning, half-baked puppy love.
A surrogate Daddy to fuck in the
hardness of things, a most private
compact with depravity.
Her love a haunted pit, and
going there with her, stupid.

Stupid with pity, stupid with
love. A fool's errand, singing into hell,
with other souls quaking, cowering,
wailing, hungry for blood. The
ghosts of fathers, mothers, lovers, rapists,
casual encounters, the girl you kissed at recess,
the boy you let touch your breast at the dance,
all await.

But I've had all I can stand. I won't
let her come back. Because: I cannot
promise anything to anyone any longer.
I'm wasted of trust, robbed of pity,
and of so much else, while she walks
the streets of the damned city, immune.

Bags
of sweet poison slung on each
shoulder, delicious with stink, and
putrefaction. Stained black. She stops,
sits quietly near the broken wall,
the burning roof and tower,
and she hugs them, as if they were
treasures to her. Family heirlooms,
last night's deposit slip,
more valuable by far than life,
than safety, than kindness, than truth,
than me.

They smell of brimstone
and plain death.
And she. And I. And others still,
all need an airing, and all need a bath.

2004

The Bar Scene

Clearer in the window than the
vague stirring shapes.
above the bar.
Deeper, too. I'm looking there at a woman,
and she is looking at me
looking at her,
but neither of us is really looking
at anyone at all.
Hat tricks with
shadow and light
to fool children.

Music lisps
a melody so beautiful.
My ears are plugged with wax.
It keeps out
the singing,
keeps me safe.

Turn off the sound, please.
Put on the subtitles.
Lash me tight to the stool,
and bring me a drink. A strong one.
Several strong ones.
Because there is
elsewhere, the weight of a crowd
roaring, a team
winning, a team
losing. And there is
hysteric laughter, of mouths
I cannot see,
shrieking from the TV.

2004

Prognostications

I was running at sixty,
and barely keeping pace, while
he rode the closed tailgate of the truck
in front of me, one leg flung over,
his foot on the bumper, as if
anything like a faulty latch or a bump
could not be. His long hair
flailed the air like a dog's ears.

To the right, a trailerful of horses
towed by a pickup pulled even with us, then
ahead; with my window down,
the sharp, ammoniac smell was overpowering,
and to the left, a semi gained on all.

I watched, white-knuckling
the steering wheel, and knew
his body would
tumble down murdered
to the pavement
any moment,
blossom in a bloody flower,
a portent rolling through
the traffic, shredded of clothes,
a bare stripped spectacle,
penis dangling,
everything we would not know
if we could not know it, out in plain sight,
a scream bleeding.

Until the truck passed us,
and I passed them.
One horse, a roan, mane fluttering,
beautiful, stared at me
between the slats of the trailer.
I looked in the rearview once.
I never saw any of them again.

2004

A Brief Disquisition on the Meaning of Life

It's all in the obsessive search for meaning,
he told her. She kicked off her shoes. We
encounter a void. Our lives are empty, he said,
as she stepped out of her pants. He sat on the bed
watching. Our lives, he said, are a spiritual vacuum,
and we seek obsessively to fill it. She was
undoing her blouse, and kicked aside the
black lace panties. You could say, he said, that
all our megaluxuriant consumer culture is one
long and ultimately futile resistance to this lack
of meaning. She shrugged off the black satin brastraps,
and twirled the bra back to front. The center, he said
heavily, not only cannot, but did not hold. The bra
fell lightly to the floor, and she was naked. So we
eat, he said, or read, he said, or get preached to, he
said, or alter our mental states in whatever
multifarious ways, he said. Grasping desperately for
some meaning to impute to this ghastly. Three-ring.
Circus. Of scoundrels and fools and clowns, parading
before us daily, on a 40-inch HD screen, or larger. And she
climbed into the other bed, where the guy with
metallic blue hair and a rabbit bone jammed through
his nasal septum patiently awaited, smiling.

2005

A Balancing of Accounts

My brother died of cancer, in the brain.
A terrible death, ugly, but not slow.
The tumor grew like a mushroom,
insidious in that dark inwardness,
pressing one side of his brain, while the opposite
side of his body twitched like a shocked frog
with each jab—*you're dying, you're dying.* And
while he was dying, his ex-wives
one by one came by—Esther, Miriam, and Ruth,
last, second, first, in that order
—each striving for their own peace,
I am sure, and each trying, in her own
particular way to make a peace with him
to get it. A kind of send-off, I think,
like a last secret fun-fuck for old time's et cetera,
just before the divorce is final, and he
—well, he gave them what they wanted.
I don't know why. I would not have.
It was the last one leaving, Ruth, who smiled
over her shoulder at him, pleased to have
got off so easy, I guess, as who would not be?
How dare to hope? To plan?
She vanished, as people will, out the door,
swallowed by time. Space. Rushing off
to new sins, and as she left, my brother grabbed
me by the arm, pulled me down to where he lay,
shrunk to sheets and a pillow, and whispered to me
urgently, hey, hey, don't tell
Esther that Ruth came by, I might be able to use all
this—the so-pregnant gesture, then, at the hospital
room—to talk her into getting back together with me.

2005

Blank Sonnet

In flash flood, the water sluices over an earth
like stone. Fire thirsts for water. There are clouds
on the far horizon, clean, and full of everything
that wicks up from salt seas. I must remember
what has been born hard is not always
bitter, like the breath of God's passing.
Pass on. I could step outside these walls
and slabs of gross flesh, and float away. West
toward the sun. Do maidens await me there?

Let the waste within be soaked with tides,
the flinty sand and obsidian shards
stroked smooth with water. I am too long
an anchorite at dry prayers, lost in the
hermitage of time.

2005

A Marriage Poem

I cannot say what love is. I know
It is the lounging
on a disordered bed, pillows flung
about carelessly, sheets in disarray,
blanket and bedspread
mountain and valley
Still warm but
heat spent.

Do not forget memory.
Somewhere the earth quakes.
The magma is rising. Great slabs and oblongs
cling and push.
A turmoil risen into light
From what is black
never to be known.

It is a flower
I have impaled.
Gorgeous with color.

2005

A Sunday Stroll in the Shambles

Something has gone away from me. Was it a bid for pity?
Always a sponge for that, but you are mistaken, I think.
If that is *what* you think, then call it an exorcism. *Something* has
    been gutted,
and it lies on the floor all wet, a distaff burden of guilt and
    responsibility.

Who *is* responsible for offal? The rain of flotsam used for your own
purposes, bearing the burden in your stead, just like Jesus looking
    up,
at how long it took you to tell even that much truth. Now you may
    die, my son.
Take your own losses: so much less than you have induced
in all these others here about. Send the cost or bear it. It *was*
you put us in harm's way—how could you *not* know? None of this
is real. God help the next fool. Some sort of pissing contest,
like boys arm-wrestling, in the end only more of it: numbing,
    disabling pain.

Remade myself, I did; escaped my demons. I thought. Endured
    shame.
Believed I would have it all, thank you.
No physical hazard could stop it,
no moral onus prevent it. These strangely articulate dreams
    beyond and behind,
that never speak of the trick it is to be able to move *out* of the
    dream,
and into the light. A glib response. One's own bankrupt account.

Art as a kind of sin, all beautiful in its terror.
Save sleep, drunkenness, the dark of night.
And *do* thank God as well,
when you see him, for drunken incompetence, a boon,
and a benison.
None of this is real.
And death does draw water.

2006

The Mystics of Water and Stone

On the horizon, an island smokes dimly.
Is it a burning bush? Salt seas
of pearl and amethyst, lapis lazuli,
turquoise, the mural
girdling the planet, broken alone
by the hard mystics of stone.
Birds or fishermen
lashing the water for food,
might dream themselves replete,
while below,
in the milky, speckled dark,
a nude husk lingers on its fragile stalk,
starved. Starving.

Just here, where the reef
anchors the sea to the rock, the
ocean of all tears sways
with the tumbling of planets,
moons, asteroids, stars.
Never forgetting the cries of the gulls,

that pick in whispered agonies
of feathers and light
bones fresher still.
A crust of truth to take off the sand,
and gnaw quietly; but we gobble all down,
all down. Tumults in rocky places,
known before. Rooted brutally to stone,
so near the slate-gray sea.

2006

Marcel Marceau Speaks to the New World Order.
Thousands Applaud.

I am made dumb.
The spectacle that passes by
unblinking
the spectacle that cowers,
whimpers.
The body of Christ himself,
broken in gutters,
every day,
pedestrian,
spurned by all but
random trash
and the ubiquitous rats.

A terrible beauty
coils
not striking but struck
at the core of all that was, is
of all that was, is
of our stifling,
unmemorable fear.
Cruel.
Banal.
Senseless, so I
make no sense of it.
No sense can be made of it.

I would set a light to silence,
and watch the world burn
entire.

2007

Absolution

It gives us everything, then takes it all.
It is said to fly, but my father
said they were not making
enough of it. Instead of into a mirror,
we should preen in a clockface,
one mask, into the masks we wear
searching for answers
and hiding from them.
Give back off the glass
ourselves alone, divided
into equal parts, falling.

Its children, its heirs,
its provisional keepers,
its victims. We prick ourselves
on its needle. Do we not bleed?
Though a stitch in it is also said
to save
something or other,
I guess because it rhymes. We
make our days within it,
old women embroidering doilies.
Patching up the always needful blanket,
for the cold. Sewing
a full suit of clothes,
to cover the shame.

2007

Triage

A song to the blackrich ruin
smouldered and stank on the altar.
Do you call for a science
better than that?

The one with the broad grin draws water
in the evening. An artifice of love.
Cleverer crafts, more ardent,
the more earnest tangle
that could never balance the loss,
teeters to the purer vision.

A better triage
of the heart. A better assay
to separate ore from dross
before excavations begin.
To economize, you know.
To avoid embarrassments,
cross-jurisdictional disputes

like this one. God's little jokes are
always the funniest,
built right into the woof,
like leprosy,
the warp, like
fundamentalism,
genocide,
greeting cards

2009.

The Terrible Beauty of Fire

Unblinking. Cowers.
Whimpers.
The body of Christ himself,
broken in gutters,
the everyday every day,
pedestrian,
spurned by all but
random trash,
and the ubiquitous rats.

A terrible beauty
coils
not striking but struck
at the core of all that was, is
of all that was, is
of all our cruelties,
memorable and unmemorable alike,
stunning in breadth, or merely
senseless. Banal.
So I make no sense of it.
No sense can be made of it.
And as a matter of recompense,
I set a light to silence,
and watch the world burn entire.
A light to warm its passing.

2009

Textures of Betrayal

You are torn as I am.
The ghosts you pursue,
ghosts of youth.
To recapture that vanished past.
Time is the force that tugs us on:
simple anger; the sting of being wronged
so profoundly, being
torn between what you seek
and all of lost time. The terrible burden
of resentment without blame.

You can tell me if I'm wrong.
But I am not wrong.
Close it off.
Stop hurting at me.
Heal. You think the clock
is ticking so fast. You think you must
make up for something, for
all you feel you have missed
with what time you have left.
I think what you will find instead is a truth.
That you can't unlearn what
you have learned, and so you can't
go back. It just won't happen. It all just
gets further and further away.

Time weighs on us both.
What do any of us know?
We do something awful
to go somewhere wonderful, but
in the end,
you're still on your back,
staring at your hands, and crying: useless.
Useless.

2009

We All

Fuming stink and turmoil,
not a sound in the room. Nothing
but dust motes in sunbeams, that fade
slowly into dusk, night, darkness.
I come and go like a wraith
to the places I must.
I stare at the pictures of my dead family.
I want nothing more than to join them.
It sounds so stupid when I say it.
I am trying to find a way to make
forgiveness hold. Still, no one put me here.
This place has been waiting for me, like a fat,
drooling spider, since the day I was
born. It has found me at last.

No pain. A valedictory.

I had a friend once who told me
he owned a suicide note, left by
some anonymous pilgrim
whose name I never knew.
He wouldn't show it to me.
I wondered even then:
how do you own that?
"Well, God, I stand before you," my friend said
the pilgrim said. My friend is one more lost
in the seas of time. I lost track of him years ago.
How much more lost the pilgrim of whom he spoke?
Time will close over us like water,
and it will be as if we never lived
soon enough. We stand on
the brink of nothing.
No reward, no punishment,
nor judgment either.
Death will bring not even knowledge,
but it could bring an end to pain.

I mean to indict no one for being young,
and hungry. Cruel, stupid, useless as that is.
I could not keep from it, I pitied her so
and was so grateful,
and that was one more failure.
It was a crime to use you that way.
To keep this beast from my door. But now
I do not know what to do.
It isn't you that eats me from the inside out.
It is my own despair, the shell of wanting and knowing
and wanting to know I have never been able to crack.
I am an egg, crimson with blood curdled in
the yellow center. I could live or die
not hungry. Sated on grief and loss. It seems as if
everything I've loved has gone away from me,
leaving me fat with sorrow and satisfied, somehow,
with my own desolation. How could it
ever have been any different? Now.

Imagine: Why?

2009

A Brief Lecture

"Cunt" was an Old German word,
not related to Latin "cunnus,"
that had not a single negative connotation.
It was the word for "female genitals," inclusive.
The closest non-pejorative equivalent now
is probably "vulva."
But about your little romance, for all
I know blissfully ongoing.
I doubt you will find much bliss anywhere.
The breakup was amicable, you say?
Then reconcile with this: I love those sorts of
rhetorical questions that answer themselves.
Don't you?
Whatever the Puritan neuroses,
aggravated by an . . .
unhappy . . . sexual history,
of which *you* are a victim,
I am one goat more unblemished.

Is that what *commitment* means?
Imperfect, inconsistent, with missteps,
grotesque errors, all human frailty intact,
good—bad—indifferent,
sacrificing some of my own,
to stick so resolutely with all
those lies I told you.
Save you the pain of the truth. See?
But people have this insane need to be abused.
Yes?
We call it the truth only
in our better moments.

I did not latterly serve that purpose well,
And so: who will cheat or abuse or otherwise
confirm you in your suffering now?
Lost little girl,
most people ultimately learn from their fuckups.
Have you?

I put them on to you, all right.
I figured you had done it, after all, and it
still seems likely: You've done worse for lovers before—
haven't you? A narcissistic cunt in love with a
narcissistic bastard. Not once but twice,
and so will it be again.

But I don't have the access
to hack the true extent of your
corruption, or your
real education. You were certainly very good in bed.
I misuse the word nonetheless, in the too-common
manner, just because I thought—no, *hoped*—
it would hurt you. Did it?
I'd like to know.
I could not get in, despite my
best intentions. Insufficient lubrication?
I do not delight myself in this.
It is a hurtful thing, to have your ruin
paraded before you. You'd know that by now.
Yes? Not so marked a contrast as
I might want to claim. And you,
a faithless, lying cunt,
unblemished.

2009

Ferris Wheel

As tall as the top of the world
might be. But you know, love's no more
a charm than that,
to lay demons.
A question in the end
of what is bartered, traded,
ransomed, lost in the partaking of
those smooth, efficient thighs,
that silk-soft mouth,
that wet tongue.

Then, too, what fire ever burned
without leaving a trace? In the
cloak room, with the cloaks,
it was made tender,
all beseeching strokes and sighs.
Red faced and bloody limbed and
blue-in-blue staring eyes—will these
winnow salvage from a dead loss?

2009

He Will Stay

So it's true. He *will* stay 'til you come.

And I know now what I should
have known before. My life
is a disease, and some aches
just don't find a cure.

Policy, as always, put
a better face on it.
Who knows what secrets
are hidden in the temple,
any temple, anywhere?
The staff makes
it look good. As good as it
might look. As good
as it could. The well-spun
particulars. But Lazarus.
He *had* to know, with all to do
all over. To live
and die.

2009

Pierce Inverarity Carries the Mail

The anonymous plinth is lain,
And so begins an epoch.
Precambrian seas, sterile with heat
precipitate layer on layer,
each as magic as malicious, unknown
unknowable, unknowing,
an index formed from grief to grief,
entablatures of failure,
all losses calibrated to the single
catalogue of waste.
She will see it all
through the lenses of her tears.

Having died,
the silence will be absolute.
We dead do not complain,
anticipate,
wonder,
groan,
or await.

What would I say to God,
enthroned in glory?
Or sleeping in an alley
with his rag of cloth,
his crust of bread,
his bottle of sweet red wine?
Step into the shade with me, I'd say.
Oh maker of promises.
I have a bone to pick with you.

2010

What Was Best

What was best,
was that the door to your room
was also the door to mine.
Ever up, ever down, all around,
the blood of millions
and the single flower,
as has been asserted by those
who should know, by-product
of my too-populous dreams.
Proud owner of the heart
gnawed so savagely by passing dogs.

2010

Epithalamium

The journey to death is a long one
Punctuated with smaller ones
Bigger
Better
That explode in the head and loins
Like flowers
Like hand grenades
That whisper like the slave
Never forget
Like the traitor heart
Never remember.

Do they come to prepare us?
Or only to press home the cruelest promise
Made all unknowing in the dark.
I would relish my first time
Again all over
All things new
No age, no aches
No morning of
The end of time
No sagging, no decay
No stealing, insidious dullness
Of mind or eye.
Live forever
Forget everything
Remember all.

2011

Becket

The sun streams down through the glass.
Dust afloat in a slanted column of light,
the center beribboned with smoke of
incense. It looks enough to stand a pillar.
Support of the world. But there: it did not hold.
Forehead, mouth, heart: *mirabile dictu,*
bread and wine together,
heart unto heart. Poor Henry.
Will no one rid me of this troublesome priest?

The dead, mouthing words—
he cannot hear them. The people content enough:
fat, silent, sated. Killings by the coffinsful, all done
in good behalf, and all to silence;
roars do not echo in the stadium,
consent nor refusal either one. Not hot,
not cold. Room enough for all.
An affluent limbo of tacit permissions.
Slay him for the bishop, prelate, deacon, baron,
king; and watch the contented cows chew slowly
the cud of it. Staring intently at that
sparkling, chattering eye.

And lo! His brains poured out like
holy waters, red all down
the richness of brocade and applique. Heavy, stiff
fabric of chasuble, cassock, miter worked
in jewels and silver and gold. He sighed once,
it is said, then turned all mute
to stone. One monument is
as pointless as any other, you know.
Memento mori, ceteris paribus.
But come. As it was said.
This fellow isn't getting up again.
Let's go.

2011

The Essential Voyeur

Cheerleaders for old, leering death, all the same to *him*,
the furry rodents, in numbers large as any,
ascurry to the precipice, clutching
cellphones, iphones, HHDs. A TV
for the essential voyeur.
Madge, the neighbor's wife
astraddle the frantically pumping thighs.
Another with stacks and stacks of magazines,
bare breasts, roseate nipples, the money shot in close-up.
There's one driving a BMW.
Doesn't know it's just not *de riguer*
any more. Too nineties,
but there you are,
over the edge with a well-engineered purr,
all the way down trailing pale smoke. He gripped
a suitcase trailing hundred dollar bills,
one of these rolled to a tube, and
dangling coyly from the nose,
fashion-statement-and-suicide-in-one,
over the edge with a shriek
gearshift agrip in one mighty paw.
Plummets to the sand below.
Thud and blood.
        Ah, me,
sad hours just aren't long enough
any more.

2011

Wreckage of Ilium

Like flames under the skin,
a spirit of heat
that will not outlive me. Fat sprites
wielding spiked bats wired for sound,
dazzling down the nerve ends: What
pain there is, there must be,
my anchor, my tether,
the watch that keeps me in the night,
knowing I will stand my post.
Come, boon companion.
When the sun paints the sky in the east,
we will see what Homer saw.

2011

Requiem Mass 1

Piggish glint in the empty eyes,
the smiling, sweaty coach.
Shiny mute whistle
between the teeth.
Crucifix aglint on the jersey.
An autumn sun.
The end of something.
Rex tremendae,
a good drill sergeant, like
all the snarling nuns
in your life. Fodder to feed the
grinning rat, that coils
its naked, pink tail, here.
About my heart.
For all is not well.

2012

Requiem Mass 2

Tuba mirum, Sister Agnes.
For all the courage
I lack. The Day of Wrath
is nigh. Today we will
see Death a-tip-toe
go past the well
Ingemisco
with his sodden gourd,
his lame jokes,
his eternal grin.

2012

Requiem Mass 3

Lacrimosa!
Save me from kindness.
From all the good women, who
give the only answer,
the spongy soft breast
I suckle in horror.
Beatific smile, scrabbling
soricine claws
sunk deep in the back.
A game for two,
a *pas de deux*.
Satan bowls with Daddy.

2012

To George, with Love

I can never recall him without his strangeness. His uniqueness, if you will. Did he possess it from birth, or did it only come to him latterly? I do not know. Now, it is unknowable. It was in 1965 when George figured out before anyone the resonant properties of the book vault of your standard sheetmetal public school desk. He played "Wipeout" on it with ferocity and violence. He was fast and precise and how it boomed. The method was to tip it over, hold it there with your legs, and go apeshit on the solid metal side. It spread wildly amongst the boys. The girls loved it; it became a sign of a certain sort of new virility. The open side of that vault acted like a megaphone, announcing this. George was a hero; the faculty was outraged.

2022

To George, with Love and Squalor

Anticipating lunacies to be, my chum.
Only there we were all children,
and with leisure that knew nothing
and gave nothing away.
The patented adolescent smirk
that knew not a thing,
and gave not a thing away.
Stifled laughter all.
Oversweet cereal munched before
the fount of that wheezing chortle;
Saturday morning wisdom.
Monkeys and stooges and men.
Was there death from the sky, then?
That might fall anywhere, and blossom
with the strangest orange flowers.
Leftovers of a rat murdered by an owl.
No greater beast than that, yet
that is the one still slouching toward
tomorrow's time and tonight's
half-slumber. Yes, that Bethlehem. Those
emblematically adolescent hungers,
protesting only their own want of orgasm
in the correct locus.
On the principle that one requires the thicker quid
for the quicker spurt. Oh God, is
this dying? Yes. Yes, it is.
And living, too if only in the smallest ways.
Yet one can continue to hope.

Today, a scam is so much more than
likely. But then, we might've been
anything at all. Giants. Assassins.
It was a narrow, seeking face
with hooded, distrustful eyes.
Is it scoliosis? Or did you never have
a backbone? Whatever, the twist is in.
I need the warp and the woof, the
predicated loom of old women making

quilts in a frame. They will use
the wedding ring pattern.
Leaving us all to wonder aloud:
what waspish predator is this?
The prey quickly stilled of its convulsions.
Beheld with all eyes, the atrocity is
in its consumption. Its termination
spawned in that terrible violence of
surviving. Yet somehow, indolent also.

Spurned somehow. Lay on, good Simpleton,
we are yet too wise for sainthood. My bodiless
lust cries on for its own temerity. Row on,
you happy, heroic dead. That murderous
bureaucracy will keep track of us yet.

2022

Burnt Offerings

Walls are only dust, temporarily perpendicular.
They will crack in time,
settle askew; a fissure open
in the midst of things.
Ardent hearts on an altar,
burnt offerings, heat but no light,
light but no heat. He was right, you know.
Not one stone will stay
where we put it.

At the turnstile, fishermen count up
the day's pile of picked bones, casting
tomorrow's nets. God is long on silence,
and fond of the ambiguous retort,
apt to take all we offer with no more
than a wink and a nod,
sufficient to the blind horse.

The stark, sheer terror of being alive
and in the world,
and subject to flesh and devil alike
makes appetite easeful altogether.

How does the heart, so bitten, hang on?
Tooth marks in the ventricles,
The septum gnawed clean through.
The blood drums in my ears. There is fear enough
in a handful of dust, and thus
we are unmade.

But I have you.
And so I know there is that,
which crosses oceans,
overthrows mountains,
shatters boundaries.
Each day, a new year upon us.

I will stay with you, my love,
and you with me.
The rest must burn as they please.

2022

Cold Snap

What a gray day. The sky
like a shawl drawn tight on the shoulders.
A brown puddle, lightened
in the first flush of a dim day. While eastward,

a smear of arterial light
blushes on the rotund water tower,
paints the windmill that sits on stilts
spinning at leisure in the wind. Shades the white clapboard
across the way, while the same wind ruffles my hair.

The light calls it up, as surely as the earth moves. And a
green carpet belies the chill.
I and you must have the both. The light that cries us
upward. The dark that drags us down.

2022

Afterword

I hope these poems work. These, however good or bad these may be, have been one of my primary means of coping with—*all that*. For a long time now. I *am* involved in mankind, you see? And herein I grieve and decry and protest and stare in horror, and also, celebrate and ennoble and lust and embolden, and try to live well from one moment to the next as best I can, and as my Grandpa Fenn used to say, "That's all a mule can do." I hope this slender volume finds its way into the hands of readers who will, if my thinking strikes its target and my writing is sufficiently coherent, understand it, and be as enlarged thereby as I have been writing it, and much better still, reading the work of those others who came before me. Back to the beginning.

Kevin M. Clay
Arlington, Texas 2025

Biography

Kevin M. Clay—Kevin Mark—was born in Fort Worth, Texas, at St. Joseph's Hospital, in 1954, to Raymond, Sr. and Edna Clay. He was educated in the public schools of the Birdville District in Haltom City, graduating from Haltom High in 1972. He married in 1976 and had two sons, Mark and Patrick, with his first wife, Selma Sherry Trantham. Twenty-four years later, beginning in 1996, he attended Tarleton University in Stephenville, Texas, transferring in with 70-odd hours from the 1970s at Tarrant County College NE in Hurst, Texas, and the University of Texas at Arlington. By 1997, he had earned Bachelor's and Master's degrees in English at Tarleton State University. In 1999, he graduated with a PhD in American Literature at the University of North Texas in Denton, Texas. Over the years, he taught at a number of institutions, including Tarrant County College NE, SE, and Downtown, Texas Wesleyan College, the University of Texas Pan-American, Paul Quinn College, South Texas College, Oklahoma State University, and Dallas College. He retired from teaching in 2021, and currently resides in Arlington, Texas with his wife, Elizabeth B. Clay.